MW00339361

A a   B b   C c

D d   E e   F f

G g   H h   I i

J j   K k   L l

M m   N n   O o

P p   Q q   R r

S s   T t   U u

V v   W w   X x

Y y   Z z

     CD-104364   I

A A A

a a

Anna

alligator

CD-104364 © Carson-Dellosa

Copy the sentence.

Anna was amazed to see an alligator in Adam's aquarium.

Trace and write the letters. Trace and write the words.

B B

b b

Bonnie

bubbles

CD-104364

Bonnie blew bubbles
beside the bus.

Trace and write the letters. Trace and write the words.

C C

c c

Candice

carnival

Copy the sentence.

Candice Caterpillar
crawled to the
carnival for cotton
candy.

Trace and write the letters. Trace and write the words.

D D

d d

Dion

doughnuts

Copy the sentence.

Dion Dog ate dozens
of delicious doughnuts.

E E

e e

Ellen

evening

Ellen Elephant ate an egg every evening for eight weeks.

Trace and write the letters. Trace and write the words.

F F
f f
Felicia
fair

 CD-104364   © Carson-Dellosa

Copy the sentence.

Felicia Flamingo saw a fancy fish at the fair.

Trace and write the letters. Trace and write the words.

G G

g g

Gavin

grapes

CD-104364

Copy the sentence.

Gavin Gorilla
gobbled the gooey
green grapes.

Trace and write the letters. Trace and write the words.

H H — — — — — —

h h — — — — — —

Henry — — — — —

hopscotch — — —

CD-104364 © Carson-Dellosa

Copy the sentence.

Henry happily played hopscotch in Hawaii.

Trace and write the letters. Trace and write the words.

I I

i i

Irene

ice-skater

CD-104364

Copy the sentence.

Irene the ice-skater
ate ice cream in
Iceland.

Trace and write the letters. Trace and write the words.

J J J

j j j

Jayla

jelly fish

CD-104364

Copy the sentence.

Jayla the jazzy jellyfish loved her job as a jeweler.

Trace and write the letters. Trace and write the words.

K K

k k

Kenyon

kittens

 CD-104364

Copy the sentence.

King Kenyon kept his kittens and kangaroos in the kitchen.

Trace and write the letters. Trace and write the words.

L L

l l

Leo

leaped

 CD-104364

Copy the sentence.

Leo Leopard leaped over lots of lemons.

Trace and write the letters. Trace and write the words.

M M
m m
Martin
mittens

Copy the sentence.

Martin Mouse mended many mittens on the moon.

Trace and write the letters. Trace and write the words.

N N

n n

Nina

newt

Copy the sentence.

Nina noticed her new neighbor's nice newt.

Trace and write the letters. Trace and write the words.

O O

o o

Oliver

oranges

Copy the sentence.

Oliver Octopus
offered oranges to
owls in outer space.

Trace and write the letters. Trace and write the words.

P P P

p p

Patrick

popcorn

CD-104364

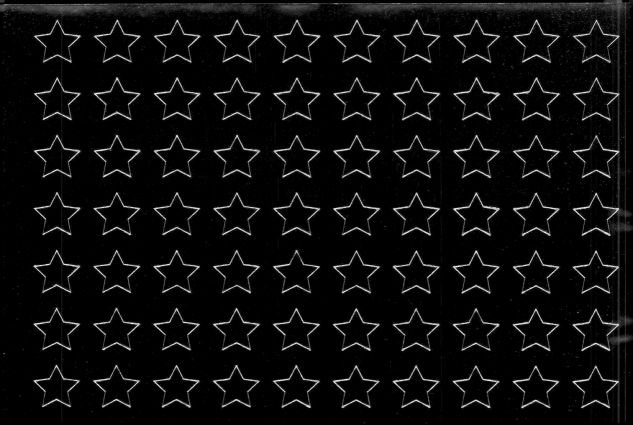

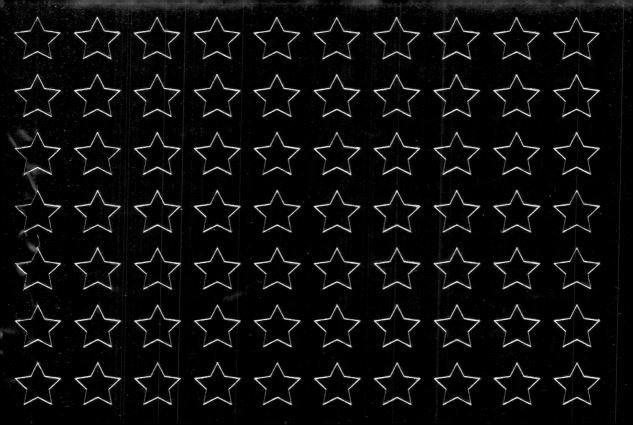

Patrick Penguin purchased pink popcorn in the park.

Trace and write the letters. Trace and write the words.

Q Q

q q

Quiana

quilt

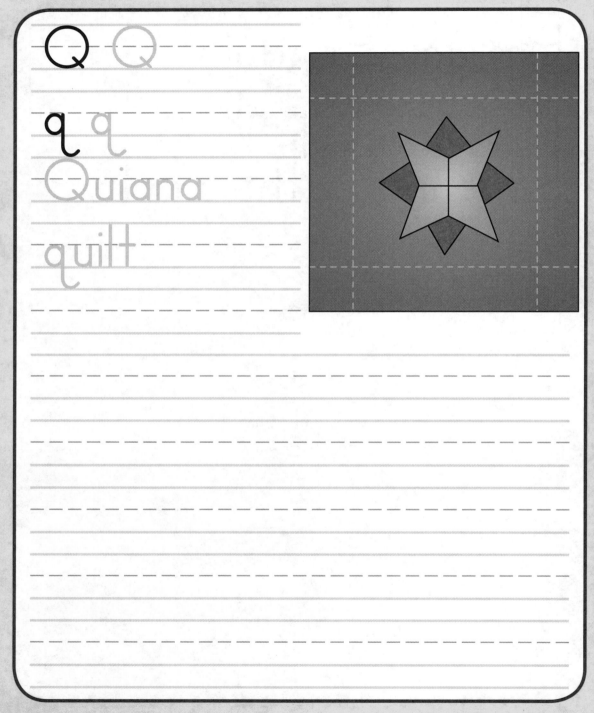

CD-104364

Queen Quiana questioned the quality of the quaint quilt.

Trace and write the letters. Trace and write the words.

R R

r r

Richard

radio

 CD-104364

Copy the sentence.

Richard Rhino raced down the ridge to recover his radio.

Trace and write the letters. Trace and write the words.

S S

s s

Samantha

sunset

 CD-104364

Samantha Snail sang softly as she set off into the sunset.

Trace and write the letters. Trace and write the words.

T T

t t

Tyler

trumpet

Tyler Turtle tried to tune his trumpet on a train.

Trace and write the letters. Trace and write the words.

U U

u u

Uma

umbrella

CD-104364

Copy the sentence.

Uma Unicorn hid under
an umbrella.

Trace and write the letters. Trace and write the words.

V V

v v

Valerie

vacation

Valerie Vulture visited a variety of vacation spots.

Trace and write the letters. Trace and write the words.

W W

w w

Wesley

weighed

CD-104364

Copy the sentence.

Wesley Walrus
weighed watermelons
on Wednesday.

Trace and write the letters. Trace and write the words.

X X

X x

Xander

examined

Copy the sentence.

Xander the expert
examined his X-ray.

Trace and write the letters. Trace and write the words.

Y Y Y

y y y

Yolanda

yodeled

Copy the sentence.

Yesterday, Yolanda yodeled, "Yoo-hoo," to Yvonne.

Trace and write the letters. Trace and write the words.

Z Z

z z

Zack

zipped

Zack Zebra zipped through the zinnias.

Trace and write the numbers and the number words.

1 — one

2 — two

3 — three

4 — four

5 — five

6 — six

7 — seven

8 — eight

9 — nine

10 — ten

CD-104364 © Carson-Dellosa

Trace and write the days of the week.

Sunday

Monday

Tuesday

Wednesday

Thursday

Friday

Saturday

Trace and write the months of the year.

January

February

March

April

Trace and write the months of the year.

May

June

July

August

September

October

November

December

CD-104364

Trace the beginning of each sentence. Then, finish the sentence.

When I am playing, I

When I grow up, I

My favorite place to
vacation is

Pretend that you are going to the grocery store. Use the words in the word bank to make a list of foods you would buy for breakfast, lunch, and dinner.

Word Bank

apples	cheese	juice	pie
bananas	chicken	lettuce	pizza
beans	cookies	macaroni	potatoes
beets	corn	milk	rice
bread	doughnuts	muffins	soup
butter	eggs	nuts	spaghetti
cake	hot dogs	oranges	steak
celery	ice cream	peaches	tomatoes
cereal	jelly	pears	waffles

Breakfast

© Carson-Dellosa

Lunch

_____

_____

_____

_____

_____

Dinner

_____

_____

_____

_____

_____

_____

Pretend that you can have any ice-cream treat you want. Use the words in the word bank to write about your favorite treat.

Word Bank

banana split	frozen	scoops
butterscotch	fudge	sherbet
caramel	marshmallow	sprinkles
cherry	milk shake	strawberry
chocolate	peanuts	sundae
cone	raisins	syrup
cookie dough	ripple	vanilla
custard	sandwich	whipped cream

CD-104364 © Carson-Dellosa

Have you been to a zoo? Use the words in the word bank to write about the animals you have seen or would like to see.

Word Bank

bear	gorilla	parrot
chimpanzee	leopard	peacock
dolphin	lion	polar bear
duck	lizard	shark
elephant	monkey	snake
emu	ostrich	tiger
flamingo	otter	turtle
giraffe	owl	zebra

Use the words in the word bank to write about your best party. Or, write about what you would like to do at your next party.

Word Bank

balloons	family	neighbors	prizes
cake	food	party	puppet
cards	friends	party hats	snacks
clown	fun	pictures	streamers
color	games	pizza	surprise
crafts	happy	play	toys
dance	ice cream	presents	wish

 CD-104364